Master the secrets of Oriental cooking...

The wok in your kitchen will serve you as a deep fryer, skillet, saucepan, soup kettle —and in a pinch, as a salad bowl. With it you can enter the world of bok choy and dow see, sesame paste and five-spice powder.

With the subtle flavors of Chinese cuisine as your reward, you will turn to your wok again and again for an experience in exotic gourmet cookery.

THE WOK
COOKBOOK

by Barbara Farr
with Irena Kirshman

Illustrations by Loretta Trezzo

Galahad Books   New York City

A native of London, Irena Kirshman has studied with master chefs here and abroad, including the Cordon Bleu School in Paris. Since 1966 she has lived in Greensboro, North Carolina, where she established a French cooking school and *La Bonne Femme*, a gourmet and gift center. She also gives television cooking demonstrations and writes articles and books on Oriental and other cuisines.

Barbara Farr teaches Chinese cooking, a long-time interest, at *La Bonne Femme* in Greensboro, N.C., and she and Mrs. Kirshman have previously co-authored a book on Oriental cookery. An accomplished artist, Mrs. Farr has set up a pottery studio at her farm, Walden 3.

Library of Congress Catalog Card Number: 76-15137
ISBN: 0-88365-159-9

Published by arrangement with Pyramid Communications, Inc.
919 Third Avenue, New York, N.Y. 10022

Manufactured in the United States of America

Contents

*Please turn the page for more
wonders of the wok*

Contents (continued)

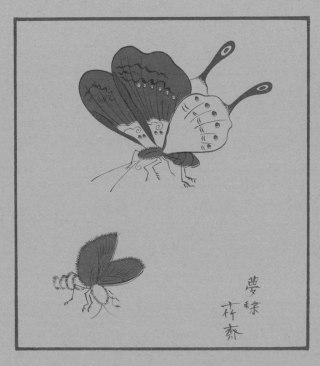

Introduction

In a country where only one-sixth of the land is arable and famines are a common occurrence, a cook must be highly skilled and inventive indeed. Chinese cooking employs every available ingredient in the greatest variety of ways. The genius of the chefs, coupled with the people's great joy in eating and highly developed aesthetic sense, has produced one of the world's great cuisines.

The two great agricultural areas of China border on the Yellow and the Yangtze rivers, and both depend upon the monsoon rains to water their crops. If the monsoon winds are weak, the Yangtze valley may be flooded, leaving no rain for the parched Yellow River. Should the winds be strong, however, they blow the rain clouds over the Yangtze and cause the Yellow River to flood. Having lived with the constant threat of flood or drought, the Chinese people are careful to waste nothing. Everything is used, and no leftovers are thrown away. Fresh fish and produce that cannot be used today are dried or pickled for tomorrow. In order to enable everyone to share in the precious meats, they are combined with vegetables. Even salt, once a most expensive luxury, is made to go farther by using soy sauce.

The variety of the food in China is infinite. There is wheat from Peking, fish from Fukien, hot peppers from mountainous Szechuan, and rice from the banks of the Yangtze and Yellow rivers. The climate varies from the extreme cold of the north where the land is frozen for eight months of the year, to the tropical heat of Kwangtung in the south. There are Buddhists in China who eat no meat and have created extraordinary vegetarian dishes, and there are nomadic Moslems who have a "campfire cuisine" based on lamb dishes. There is so little grazing land that beef-rais-

ing is almost unknown, and dairy products are seldom used. Most Chinese eat the pork, chicken, and duck that are traditionally raised at home, varying their diet with fish and shell-fish.

The characteristic, however, that sets Chinese cooking apart from all others is its unique style. Nearly all of the food is prepared in a single pot—the wok, which is a wide-mouthed, shallow metallic bowl with handles. The wok is used as a deep fryer, skillet, sauce-pan, stewpot, soup kettle, and steam bath. In a pinch, it can serve as a salad bowl or rain-hat! A Chinese cook armed with a wok and cleaver can cook virtually anything. In order to preserve fuel, which is scarce, wok cooking is a kind of shorthand, a quick way of cook-ing. It is a method that, when mastered, al-lows the lady in Canton to cook the produce from Tientsin and the lady in any kitchen any-where to make the best of everything from everywhere.

Composing A Chinese Meal

The simple, rational principle of yin-yang is the heart of Chinese philosophy. Yin is fe-male; passive; dark; even; moon and earth. Yang is male; active; light; odd; sun and heaven. As one expands, the other contracts. Though they contrast, they are dependent on each other, and they also intertwine. Because there can be no light without dark, there is a part of yin in yang and vice versa. The uni-verse, therefore, is orderly—a place of har-monious contrast, not only as a whole but within every separate part. Thus, crisp bok choy is served with chewy mushrooms; mild shrimp are combined with pungent black beans.

The secret of planning a Chinese meal is to start with the one dish that you would like to have, and then look for others which contrast harmoniously.

An important part of cooking Chinese food is to have everything ready before you start to cook. We like to arrange all the ingredients for each dish on small trays.

The very short cooking time of most dishes, and the practice of incorporating cooking or marinating liquids into delicious sauces, assures the maximum flavor and texture with a minimum loss of vitamins and minerals.

Serving Dinner

Guests are expected to share in each dish (see Menu Ideas). A round table is ideal so that each guest can easily reach each dish. When soup is on the table, the guests are urged to be seated, because in polite Chinese fashion, they take rather a long time deciding who shall enter the dining room first. Host and hostess sit with their backs to the door, facing the guest of honor. Then, all the dishes and the rice are served at once. The hostess apologizes for the meagerness of the meal (though it may be magnificent). The guests praise each dish, pointing out its virtues. All begin to eat. The hostess apologizes, the guests rhapsodize, and everyone is happy.

Each guest has before him a pair of chopsticks, a porcelain spoon, a rice bowl, a small dish for dipping condiments such as soy sauce, another small dish for the spoon to rest in, a wine cup, and perhaps a soup dish.

Holding his bowl of rice in his left hand, each diner uses his chopsticks to pluck a tidbit from one of the dishes in the center of the table. He allows a little of the sauce to drop upon his rice, and pops the tidbit into his mouth. In this manner he eats from every dish, taking a mouthful of rice when it pleases him. He samples the delicious sauces and savory soup with his porcelain spoon. To share food in this manner is far more conducive to pleasant and relaxed discussion than the western practice of hovering over one's private hoard of food!

dish, a fish dish, a chicken dish, a vegetable dish, and rice. As you can see, soup and rice are not considered main courses, and dessert is not considered at all. If meat, fish, and chicken sound like a lot for four people, remember that there is only a little of each ingredient in each dish. A single chicken, for instance, can make White Chicken with Mushrooms, Empress Chicken, and soup!

Recipe Yield: The recipes in this book will serve two (American style) unless otherwise noted.

Here and on the following pages are some possible menu combinations.

Menu Planning

A Chinese dinner consists of one main course for each guest. Thus, a dinner for two would be soup, a meat dish, a vegetable dish, and rice. Dinner for four might be soup, a meat

Dinners For 2	
Watercress Soup **Stuffed Mushrooms** **Beef with Bok Choy** **Rice** **Fresh Fruit**	**Egg Flower Soup** **Steamed Fish** **Chinese Vegetable** ** Combination** **Rice** **Honeyed Apples**

(continued)

Menu Planning *(continued)*

Dinners For 4

Watercress Soup
Seasoned Mush-
  rooms
Shu Mai
Green Pepper
  Chicken
Pineapple Pork with
  Ginger and Leeks
Rice
Almond Cookies

Wonton Soup
Shrimp with Lob-
  ster Sauce
Stuffed Cucumber
Empress Chicken
Snow Peas with
  Water Chestnuts
Rice
Sweet-Filled Won-
  tons

Velvet Corn Soup
Pearl Balls
Spring Rolls
White Chicken with
  Mushrooms
Stir-Fried Vege-
  tables
Rice
Honeyed Apples

Soup with Shrimp
  Dumplings
Steamed Spareribs
  with Black Beans
Sesame Beef
Steamed Chinese
  Cabbage
Water Chestnuts
  with Minced Meat
Rice
Ice Cream and Fruit

Dinners For 6

Noodle Soup
Deep-Fried Wontons
Stuffed Mushrooms
Empress Chicken
Sweet and Sour
  Pork
Savory Custard
Chinese Vegetable
  Combination
Rice
Almond Cookies

Celery Cabbage and
  Dried Shrimp
  Soup
Shrimp Kair-Tsup
Chicken Wings in
  Oyster Sauce
Stuffed Fuzzy Melon
  (or Cucumber)

Shu Mai
String Beans with
  Fermented Bean
  Curd
Crispy Spiced Duck
Rice
Ice Cream and Fruit

Wonton Soup
Szechuanese
  Twice-Cooked
  Pork
Shrimp with Lobster
  Sauce
Red-Stewed Beef
Stir-Fried Bok Choy
Lemon Sauce
  Chicken
Seasoned Mush-
  rooms
Rice
Fresh Fruits

Lunch Or Supper	
Spring Rolls **Curry Pork Noodles** **Almond Cookies**	**Water Chestnuts** **with Minced Meat** **Savory Custard** **Noodle Soup** **Honeyed Apples**
Chicken Wings **Stuffed with** **Smithfield Ham** **Fried Rice with** **Oyster Sauce** **Stuffed Mushrooms** **Sweet-Filled Won-** **tons**	**Shu Mai** **Egg Pockets** **Steamed Spareribs** **with Black Beans** **Fruit**

Cocktail Buffet	Buffet Dinner
Deep-Fried Won- **tons** **Spring Rolls** **Shu Mai** **Seasoned Mush-** **rooms** **Stuffed Mush-** **rooms** **Fish Puffs** **Chicken Wings in** **Oyster Sauce** **Pearl Balls** **Sweet-Filled Won-** **tons**	**Three Precious** **Fried Rice** **Snow Peas with** **Water Chestnuts** **Fish Puffs** **Chicken Wings** **Stuffed with** **Smithfield Ham** **Stuffed Cucumber** **Sweet and Sour** **Pork** **Pearl Balls** **Fresh Fruits**

Utensils And Methods

THE CHINESE CLEAVER is the most versatile of kitchen tools, and mastery of it eliminates the need for most other knives. The blade, kept sharp as a razor, will slice meat and vegetables paper-thin. The flat side of the blade is excellent for crushing garlic cloves and for scooping up chopped ingredients and carrying them to the wok. The fat back of the blade is an effective tenderizer, and the handle is a good pestle for pulverizing.

If the food you are going to slice tends to roll away, hold it between the thumb and forefinger of your left hand. Do not extend the forefinger, but tuck it under to steady the food. In this way you are protecting those tender fingertips. With your right hand, grasp

The wok consists of a wide, shallow pan with handles. It sits on a metal ring and may be topped with a fitted cover for simmering or a bamboo steamer.

the handle of the cleaver, extending your forefinger along the back of the blade. Hold the blade at an angle, and chop with short, firm motions. The knife is heavy—let **it** do the work!

Meat is easier to slice very thinly if it is partly frozen—just chilled enough to offer a little resistance to the knife. It should not be as hard as a brick! After a few tries, you will be able to tell when it is frozen (or thawed) enough.

THE CLEAVER

SHREDDING is accomplished by dividing slices into "matchsticks."

MINCING is chopping the shreds into tiny pieces. We like to mince meat by using two cleavers, one in each hand.

TO CHOP through bone, raise the cleaver to shoulder height, then bring it down rapidly with a snap of the wrist. Even spareribs can be chopped in this way. You will become accurate quite quickly, but **please** keep your left hand away.

DEEP-FRYING: A crisp, golden outer surface contrasting with a moist, tender morsel inside is a taste sensation produced only by deep-frying. To achieve this result, it is important to pay heed to all the "rules," or you may find yourself eating cold, greasy, soggy food, which will be a disaster of unmitigated proportion. It is often helpful to make use of a thermometer to check the temperature of the oil.

Fry only a few pieces at a time. Crowding

DEEP-FRYING

RED-STEWING simply means cooking in water with soy sauce. If salt were added instead of soy sauce, it would be white-stewing. Because red-stewing is used for large pieces of meat and takes a long time, it is seldom found on restaurant menus. Only a little of the broth is served with the meat, and the rest is saved to be used in your next red-cooked dish. It keeps well if used every week; otherwise, it may be frozen and used any time.

Red-stewing is the method most often used for cooking cheaper cuts of meat. The meat is cooked for a relatively long period of time until it is tender.

STEAMING is a means of cooking food with moist heat. Food is placed in a perforated pan over boiling water. A lid over the perforated pan allows the steam to pass over and around the food. Sometimes the food is placed directly on the perforated pan as for Shu Mai, sometimes in a bowl or plate that is smaller than the perforated pan, so the steam can circulate freely. In China the most common and most attractive steamer is formed by a wood-

the pan will lower the temperature of the oil, and the food will not crispen.

Tongs, a wire strainer, or chopsticks will be needed to remove and drain hot food. A wok is an excellent utensil for deep frying because very little oil is needed and the thin sides allow the heat to be regulated. Used oil may be saved and reused. To prevent flavors lingering, clear the oil by adding a few slices of ginger and frying for two or three minutes.

Strain used oil through a fine strainer lined with cheesecloth.

RED-STEWING

STEAMING

en hoop surrounding a woven bamboo base. It fits neatly into a wok, and several steamers can be stacked up on the same wok. If you don't have a bamboo steamer, a perforated pie plate that will sit on a wok can be used. A homemade steamer can be made from a small tin can supporting a large pot lid, or simply place the plate of food directly on the can. Add boiling water to the wok, keeping it below the level of the plate. Cover the wok and—voila—a steamer!

Food that is steamed will be tender and juicy, so this method is often used for cooking delicate foods such as fish. As Chinese home cooking traditionally does not include an oven, breads, pastries, etc., are "baked" in a steamer.

STIR-FRYING is a technique that is wholly Chinese. Food is cut into rather small pieces and tossed in hot oil in a heated wok. Because so much of the surface of the food comes in contact with both wok and oil, the food cooks very quickly without sticking to the sides of the wok. The wok must be heated

STIR-FRYING

before the oil is added. Foods are added in a certain order so that nothing will be over-cooked. Common sense will dictate the sequence. Flank steaks will take longer to cook than peas. So the steak is added to the wok before the vegetables. Heavy–stemmed vegetables, such as celery cabbage, are added before the thin bean sprouts.

Longer-cooking vegetables, such as carrots, can be parboiled, then stir-fried. Toss-cooking is another word for stir-frying and is an accurate description of the technique. The food is kept in motion with an action somewhat between tossing a salad and beating eggs. The easiest method of stirring is with chopsticks. The long handles do not get hot, and the soft wood will not break the ingredients as they are cooking.

It is the many stir-fried dishes which have made Chinese food so popular. As each ingredient is stir-fried to its individual peak of perfection, the results can be sensational. The basic idea of combining a little meat with one or two vegetables makes vegetables espe-

Lifting garlic out of wok with chopsticks

Mushrooms soaking

Mixing cornstarch paste

cially delicious, even to those who usually scorn them. It makes a little meat go a long way, too!

Many people hesitate to try Chinese cooking because they fear they will need too many exotic, expensive, and hard-to-find ingredients. This is not true. A most basic list of what is needed for Chinese cooking would be:

Peanut oil	Any fresh, leafy
Salt	vegetable
Wine	Any meat or fish
Cornstarch	Eggs
Sugar	Poultry
Garlic	Scallions

Soy sauce should be included, but if it is not available, you may increase your salt very slightly. Fresh ginger root should also be included, but if you can't find it, just omit it.

The "exotic" ingredients are not expensive and are readily available by mail. Most of those which would be considered staples in a Chinese kitchen can be kept a long time and are used in fairly small quantities. Also, some Chinese ingredients are finding their way to the shelves of supermarkets and fancy food stores.

Perhaps the most important ingredient in Chinese cooking is ingenuity. If a recipe calls for spinach and you don't have spinach, you should try any leafy vegetable you have handy. If your recipe calls for beef and you only have chicken—go ahead anyway, just keep in mind that chicken has a more delicate flavor than beef, and adjust your seasonings accordingly. Whatever it is you lack for your recipe, let it inspire you to improvisation, rather than discourage any attempt.

Shopping Guide:
Fresh Foods Available In Chinese Groceries

BEAN CURD

Bean curd is a "cheese" derived from soy beans. It is white, soft, and creamy, with a very bland flavor. It can be eaten plain, with accompaniments, stewed, steamed, or fried. It will keep a few days in water in a covered container. The canned variety can be used in soups and stews. It is available by the piece in Chinese and Japanese groceries.

BEAN SPROUTS

Two varieties of bean sprouts are available, the tiny mung and the large soy. We prefer the mung, as they do not have the raw bean flavor sometimes encountered in the soy sprout. These crispy sprouts lend a delicate flavor to many dishes. Available by weight in Chinese and Japanese groceries, they may be

kept refrigerated a few days in a plastic bag. The canned variety is a rather poor substitute.

BOK CHOY

Bok choy has thick white stems and bright green leaves. The long stems are softer in texture than celery, and not stringy. It is fairly bland in flavor. Small bok choy, when available, is called choy sahm. It can be bought in both Chinese and Japanese markets by the "head," and it keeps like celery. A combination of spinach and celery could be substituted. Bok choy may be refrigerated in plastic wrap for about one week. Cook as Chinese cabbage, spinach, or Swiss chard. This is a good salad vegetable.

CHIVES, CHINESE

Chinese chives, which are sold by the bunch in Chinese groceries, are more pungent than regular chives and look rather like grass. Ordinary chives can be substituted.

DUCK, ROAST

The roast ducks hanging in Chinese groceries are for sale either whole or by the quarter piece. You can warm the duck in the delicious gravy that comes with it, and serve it as is, or use it in other dishes. The grocer will chop the duck or not, as you wish.

EGGS, PRESERVED—("hundred-year eggs", ancient eggs, and so on)—Pay dahn in Cantonese

These are eggs that have been buried in lime and clay for about one hundred days. They are eaten as a relish or hors d'oeuvre or may be added to other (usually egg) dishes. They may be kept at room temperature for several weeks. The black outer crust and the inner shell must be gently removed before the egg can be sliced with a thin, sharp knife. They can be bought in Chinese markets.

EGGS, SALT-PRESERVED—DUCK— Hom dahn in Cantonese

These eggs are used as an ingredient in many dishes, especially in steamed egg dishes. They are available in Chinese groceries. Refrigerated, they will keep about a month; at room temperature, several days.

GINGER

Fresh ginger root is one of the most important flavors in Chinese cooking. It is available in Chinese, Japanese, Spanish, and fancy groceries, and by mail. We find that it keeps for months in a ginger jar. If it sprouts, cook the tender sprouts, too. We have a friend who freezes the roots whole and cuts off a frozen slice as needed. Powdered ginger is not a substitute for fresh ginger, though you might use a very tiny pinch in a stewed dish. In most cases, if you do not have fresh ginger, it may be omitted from the recipe without spoiling the dish.

HAM, CHINESE

Used as seasoning or garnish, Smithfield ham is the closest equivalent.

LEEKS

May be refrigerated in plastic wrap for two or three weeks. Discard root and tough green leaves, and make deep slits in the green end. Wash very carefully—they will be sandy. Use instead of onions in soups and stews.

LOTUS ROOT

Lotus root is sold fresh by the pound in Chinese and Japanese groceries. It makes a crisp pickle and an interesting addition to many other dishes. Peeled and sliced, it is a most decorative vegetable.

MELON, BITTER—Foo Gwa in Cantonese

Bitter melon has a bright green, wrinkled skin and contains quinine, which gives it a bitter flavor. It is used mostly in soups. Sold in Chinese markets.

MELON, FUZZY OR HAIRY—Dick gwa in Cantonese

Scrape the fuzz of this long, thin, green melon, and it can be used in many dishes. Its flavor is rather like cucumber, which makes a good substitute. Sold in Chinese markets.

MELON, WINTER—Tung gwa in Cantonese

Winter melon is a very large melon that looks as though its dark green skin were covered with frost. In Chinese markets, it can be bought in pieces, by weight. It is an excellent soup ingredient.

MUSTARD CABBAGE—Guy choy in Cantonese

Chinese mustard cabbage is bright green with crinkly leaves and has a faint resemblance to cabbage. When cooked, it has a delicious, slightly mustard flavor. Sold in Chinese markets.

NOODLES, FRESH

Fresh noodles can be bought by the pound in Chinese groceries. They can be refrigerated a few days or frozen. Dried noodles are a poor substitute. It is not difficult to make your own, and we include a recipe.

PARSLEY, CHINESE

Sold in Spanish groceries as **Cilantro,** or fresh coriander, this spicy herb is also used in Indian and Pakistani cooking. It is used mainly as a condiment, and it can be bought by the bunch in Chinese groceries.

PORK ROAST—Char siu in Cantonese

More of a barbecued pork than a roast pork,

it is available by the pound in Chinese groceries. Roast pork is used in stir-fried dishes, fried rice, buns, soups, and as a garnish. We always buy enough to freeze in several packages, each containing about one-half pound.

SAUSAGE, CANTONESE—Lap cheong in Cantonese

This tasty sausage can be seen hanging in Chinese groceries. It is used mostly as an ingredient in other dishes, but is served alone as an appetizer. It must be cooked, usually by steaming. It keeps well at room temperature, but if kept a long time, we prefer to refrigerate it. The sausage comes in pairs, and the price is determined by weight. We have bought them by mail.

SPRING ROLL SKINS—Chung gun pay in Cantonese

These are fresh, precut noodles for wrapping spring rolls. We have given a recipe for making your own, but it is much easier to walk into a Chinese market and buy a pound. We have bought them by mail. If not used im-

mediately, fresh skins may be refrigerated a few days or frozen.

SNOW PEAS

These edible pea pods are available fresh in Chinese groceries most of the year. They are also available frozen in some supermarkets. They are usually used more as a garnish than as a major ingredient. If bought fresh, they must have the strings and stems removed and be dropped in boiling water a few seconds until the color brightens. Rinse in cold water, drain, and use immediately or freeze for future use. We freeze them in packages of six to ten pods, a handy amount for most dishes.

WATER CHESTNUTS—Mah tuy in Cantonese

Sweet, crispy water chestnuts are not always available. When they are, they are expensive and difficult to peel, but worth the effort. They must be washed well, and the brown skin removed carefully with a paring knife or potato peeler. They may be kept under water a few days in the refrigerator. They are sold by weight in Chinese markets. As for the canned variety, please see under Condiments and Staples Available in Supermarkets.

WONTON SKINS

See Spring Roll Skins.

Shopping Guide:
Fresh Foods Available In Supermarkets

ASPARAGUS

Fresh, young asparagus may be stir-fried alone or used in several delicious dishes when it is in season.

BROCCOLI

The thick stems are peeled and parboiled, then stir-fried with the tender flowerets alone or with other ingredients.

CABBAGE

White cabbage is very good stir-fried, but is

too strong-flavored to be substituted for Chinese cabbage.

CHINESE or CELERY CABBAGE

This versatile vegetable, which can be found in your local supermarket, can also be found in any Chinese market. It is the basis for many dishes, and an important ingredient in many others.

CARROTS

Carrots are used as much for their color as for their flavor. If they are to be used in a stir-fried dish, the slices must be parboiled.

CELERY

Although celery is not a Chinese vegetable, its flavor is very compatible with Chinese foods. It can be used in many ways, and it is a fair substitute for bok choy.

CUCUMBER

Cucumber is used in many Chinese dishes, and is a good substitute for fuzzy melon.

EGGPLANT

If you can find the variety of eggplant that is only finger-long at maturity, you have the eggplant the Chinese use. Otherwise, a small, ripe eggplant may be used if cut vertically into sections.

GARLIC

Garlic is a very important ingredient in many Chinese dishes, although you seldom encounter a strong garlic taste. Fresh garlic is nearly always used, seldom the powder.

LETTUCE

Shredded lettuce is a good ingredient for stir-frying and can substitute for the leafy tops of bok choy in soups and other dishes.

LEEKS

This member of the onion family is often hard to find. Anyone familiar with leeks knows that there is really no substitute, but two scallions per leek are a reasonable compromise. Only the white or palest part of the leek is used.

MUSHROOMS

White mushrooms are used in some Chinese dishes. They are not a substitute for black dried mushrooms. We have seen canned white mushrooms used in restaurant versions of Moo Goo Gai Pan, but they are not recommended.

ONIONS
Ordinary yellow onions are used in many stir-fried dishes, but are too strong to be used in steamed dishes or soups.

PEPPERS, SWEET
Sweet green peppers are used in Chinese cooking, but in most instances, they must be parboiled just until their color brightens before being added to the dish being cooked.

PEPPERS, HOT
Fresh hot peppers are called for in some dishes. They are not always readily available; canned hot, green chili peppers may be used.

SCALLIONS
Scallions are used extensively in Chinese cooking. Only the white or palest green part is used, though the tenderest part of the darker green may be used for garnishing. To "knot" a scallion, choose a thin one, trim away the root and darkest green, and draw the scallion firmly between the thumb and forefinger until it is pliable enough to tie in a simple knot. This will facilitate its final removal in long cooked dishes.

SPINACH
Alone, spinach provides one of the tastiest of simple stir-fried dishes. It is used in many other ways, too, including as a substitute for the leafy tops of bok choy.

WATERCRESS
Keep in jar with cut end in water in the refrigerator for about one week.

Shopping Guide:
Condiments And Staples
Available In Chinese
Groceries Or By Mail

FERMENTED BLACK BEANS—Dow see in Cantonese

Washed and mashed to a paste, these beans give a subtle and interesting flavor to many dishes, especially seafood. Available by weight, they may be kept under refrigeration for a long time.

BEAN CURD CHEESE—Fu yu or Fu yee in Cantonese

This is a strong-flavored, fermented bean curd product that is used as a seasoning and served in small dishes as a table condiment. Available in jars. Opened jars keep well in the refrigerator.

BEAN SAUCE—Sam see jeung in Cantonese

Available in cans by mail or in Chinese groceries, this is a salty bean paste, actually more like a bean "jam," used as a seasoning.

BEAN THREADS or CELLOPHANE NOODLES—Fun soo in Cantonese

These noodles may be deep-fried for a crispy garnish, but are most often soaked twenty minutes and then cooked as a noodle dish or in a soup. They become very mushy if not served immediately. They are available in bundles of one-eighth to one-half pound. They keep well.

CABBAGE, SALT-PRESERVED—Haahm choy in Cantonese

Salt-preserved cabbage can be bought by the piece from large vats in Chinese groceries. It also comes in jars and, after opening, it will keep a long time in the refrigerator. It is a basic ingredient in several tasty dishes.

CUCUMBER PICKLE and MIXED PICKLES

These pickles, which are available in cans

from Chinese groceries, make a fine garnish for steamed fish and other dishes. They may also be served as an accompaniment. They keep well if refrigerated in jars.

FIVE SPICE POWDER
A very subtle flavoring. The best substitute is cinnamon with a pinch each of clove and anise powder added.

GLUTINOUS RICE—Nor my in Cantonese
This type of rice is used principally in desserts and a few special dishes. Available by weight.

HOI SIN SAUCE
A thick, spicy sauce used as a condiment in many dishes, especially barbecued meats. Available in cans. After opening, it may be kept a long time in a covered jar in the refrigerator.

HOT PEPPER SAUCE
Chinese hot pepper sauce is thick and hot.

Any liquid hot pepper sauce found in a supermarket could be substituted, but the quantity should be reduced by half.

LILY BUDS, DRIED or GOLDEN NEEDLES
These are available by the pound and must be soaked and de-stemmed before cooking. They keep well in an airtight container.

LYCHEE (Litchi), CANNED
The delicate fruit of the lychee tree has a very short season, but happily is available in cans all year. May be found in some fancy groceries and supermarkets.

DRIED MUSHROOMS—Doon goo in Cantonese
Available by the pound, these dried black mushrooms must be soaked about twenty minutes and their stems removed before cooking. They are a delicious addition to many dishes, and they are the main ingredient in several. They keep well in an airtight container.

OYSTER SAUCE—Ho you in Cantonese

A thick, brown, salty oyster extract, this sauce may be used in place of soy sauce in many dishes. It has no fishy taste. Available in bottles, it keeps very well. We prefer to refrigerate an opened bottle. It is sometimes available in fancy groceries.

DRIED SCALLOPS

Dried scallops must be soaked overnight or cooked a long time. They are used mostly in soup or congee. They keep well in a covered container and are available by the pound.

SESAME OIL

This fragrant, tasty oil is available in many fancy groceries as well as Chinese markets and by mail. It is not used as a cooking oil, but as a garnish and flavoring ingredient.

SESAME PASTE

Under the name of sesame tahini, sesame paste is more often available in Near Eastern markets than in Chinese groceries. It can

also be found in some fancy groceries. You can mash sesame seeds in a mortar or substitute peanut butter!

SHRIMP, DRIED
Available by the pound, they keep well in a covered container. They must be soaked in water or wine for about twenty minutes before cooking. They have a strong flavor and are usually used as a seasoning. They may also be eaten as a snack without soaking.

SHRIMP CHIPS
Used alone as a snack or as a garnish, these chips must be deep-fried before using. They may be bought ready-to-eat, but are much more expensive. Available in boxes, they come either plain or multicolored and keep well in an airtight container.

SOY SAUCE—Light Soy Sauce—Sin chau in Cantonese
This is the sauce most often used in Chinese cooking. The term "soy sauce" in this book always refers to this light soy sauce. If you cannot get to a Chinese grocery, you may order it by mail. The only available substitute is a Japanese soy sauce that is available in many supermarkets. As for American soy sauce, use it only as a last desperate resort. If you read the label, you will find that it contains little or no soy bean!

SOY SAUCE—Dark Soy Sauce—Chau yow in Cantonese
This is a very dark, heavy soy sauce with molasses in it. Available in Chinese groceries and by mail. A good substitute is "Chinese Brown Gravy Sauce" available in supermarkets.

STAR ANISE
Star-shaped cloves, anise flavored, lend a subtle flavor to red-stewed dishes. They are available by weight and should be kept in an airtight container.

TREE EARS—Wun yee in Cantonese
Tree ears are actually a fungus, which if washed and soaked before use, lends a crunchy texture to a dish. Sold by weight, they keep well in an airtight container.

Shopping Guide:
Condiments And Staples Available In Supermarkets

ALMONDS
Toasted or untoasted, they are sometimes used as a garnish, and other times as an ingredient.

BAMBOO SHOOTS
Available in cans in Chinese groceries and supermarkets. Those from Chinese groceries are cheaper, though both are good. If you can find whole ones, they are more versatile than the sliced. After opening, the unused portion may be placed in a jar with cold water to cover and kept in the refrigerator several days.

CHILI PEPPERS—HOT
Hot green chili peppers are available in cans in most supermarkets. They are an adequate substitute for fresh hot chilies in cooked dishes, though not for pickling.

CHILI SAUCE
Used with ketchup in some sauces.

CORNSTARCH
Used as a thickening ingredient and in making noodles and wontons.

HONEY
Any good-grade, clear, pure honey can be used.

KUMQUATS
Kumquats preserved in syrup are available in jars in many fancy food stores and supermarkets as well as Chinese groceries. Used as a dessert or a dessert ingredient.

MUSTARD—HOT CHINESE STYLE
Sometimes available in jars in supermarkets, it can be made at home by adding enough water to mustard powder to form a paste. Make it as you need it; it doesn't keep.

OIL
Peanut oil is the most desirable for Chinese cooking. For deep-frying, a little lard may be added if desired.

PEPPER, BLACK

Black pepper is not used often in Chinese cooking.

PLUM SAUCE

Available in cans or jars and often called Duck Sauce, it is available in Chinese and fancy groceries and many supermarkets. Different brands vary in flavor, so try a few. It is used mostly as a dipping sauce served at the table.

PINEAPPLE

Canned pineapple chunks are handy to keep around for sweet and sour dishes and desserts.

RICE

The Chinese prefer white, long-grain rice. Brown rice may also be used.

SALT

SOY SAUCE

See Condiments and Staples Available in Chinese Groceries or by Mail.

SUGAR

Both white and brown sugar are used. White is the more important and is used in many dishes. Brown is only used when it will not spoil the color of the sauce.

VINEGAR

Vinegar used in Chinese cooking should be light in both color and taste. Our favorite is rice vinegar, which is available in Japanese and fancy groceries, but a good cider vinegar does very well.

WATER CHESTNUTS

Canned water chestnuts are available from Chinese groceries and in supermarkets. They are not a substitute for fresh water chestnuts, which are infinitely superior. The canned ones may be used to add a little textural interest to a dish, though. Unused water chestnuts may be stored in fresh water to cover in the refrigerator for several days.

WINE

Whenever we refer to wine in this book, we mean a dry, white wine. A good, dry sherry is perfectly adequate. Wine is used extensively in Chinese cuisine. We find that Japanese sake is rather too sweet.

Guide to Meat, Fish And Poultry

BEEF

The cuts of beef most used in Chinese cooking are flank steak, stewing meat, and shin. Whenever thin sliced beef is called for in a recipe, flank steak is preferred.

PORK

Because pork is the most common meat in most of China, there is almost no part of the hog for which some recipe has not been devised. We find it helpful to buy a pork loin, have it boned, and cut the meat into portion-sized chunks to be frozen. The bones are used for making stock. The frozen meat can be sliced for stir-fried dishes and soups. If the meat is cut into thick strips, rather than chunks, you can make Chinese roast pork, which may then be frozen and used in other dishes.

FISH AND SHELLFISH

Fish are used whole, filleted, and minced. Any fish is only as good as it is fresh. The same is true of shellfish. If the fish has been frozen, it is better not to use it in the dishes that call for it to be steamed or fried whole, because these call for the very freshest fish.

POULTRY

For most duck dishes, a whole duck is required. Recipes in which a frozen duck may be used are so indicated. With ducks and chickens, however, the fresher they are, the better. Because a rather small amount of meat is called for in most chicken stir-fried dishes, we find it most economical to buy a whole fryer and cut it up. The breast meat is used immediately in the stir-fried dish. The legs and thighs are frozen for use in a stewed dish. The rest of the bird, with the skin and the breast bones, goes into a pot for chicken soup and stock.

Tea

GREEN TEA

The brew is not green, but straw-colored; it is the tea itself that is "green," that is, not fermented. Among the green teas some of the best are:

Sow Mee—(Eyebrows of Longevity)—A good tea to drink in spring and summer. Good cold.

Lung So—(Dragon's Beard)—Light and pleasant.

Lung Ching—(Dragon Well)—Considered the finest green tea. It is as revered as fine wine.

SEMI-FERMENTED TEA

The tea most often served in Chinese restaurants is the semi-fermented **Oolong** (Black Dragon) tea. It is a very popular tea, good at any time of the day. **Jasmine** tea is oolong tea to which jasmine blossoms have been added, giving a delicate scent and flavor.

BLACK TEA

The fully fermented tea is called black. It makes a reddish brew.

Tit Kwan Yin—(Iron Goddess of Mercy)—The finest black tea. To be treasured and drunk as fine wine.

Lapsang Soochong—Has a definitely smoky flavor.

Keemun—An excellent black tea.

How To Brew Tea

1. Measure freshly drawn water into a pot and set over high heat to boil.

2. Measure tea leaves into a nonmetal teapot. Using 1/2 teaspoon for each measured cup of water is about right. You may use a little less for green tea. The teapot should be warmed before the leaves are added.

3. As soon as the water reaches a very strong

boil, pour it over the leaves. Let them steep 3-5 minutes. No longer.

4. After the first brew has been drunk, a second brew may be made by steeping the leaves again in freshly boiled water. Many connoisseurs prefer the second brew.

Water that has been standing too long before boiling will be flat. Water that has boiled too long will also be flat.

Although wine is the drink of ceremony and celebration, tea is drunk at any time of day, in any season, in any place. There are teashops where gentlemen gather for tea and philosophy, and it is often brewed by travelers at the edge of mountain springs. Padded baskets, in which teapots nest snugly, keep tea hot for hours.

Tea leaves should be kept in airtight containers, and used as soon as possible.

Tea should never be brewed in a metal pot as it imparts a flavor of its own and diminishes the delicacy of the tea.

Recipes for Wok Cookery

Egg Flower Soup

A classic made with simple ingredients.

8 Chinese black dried mushrooms
(optional)
6 cups Basic Chicken Broth (see
recipe on page 43)
1 cup leafy greens—spinach,
lettuce, or celery cabbage
tops—shredded

1 cup leftover meat, shredded
1 whole egg or 2 egg whites,
stirred
¼ teaspoon sesame oil
1 scallion, finely minced

Soak the mushrooms in a small bowl of warm water for 20 minutes. Discard the stems and shred the caps. Heat the Chicken Broth almost to boiling; add the greens, mushrooms, and meat. Heat until the greens wilt. Bring the soup quickly to a boil and add the egg whites while stirring vigorously. Immediately remove the wok from the heat. Garnish with the sesame oil and scallion. Serve very hot.

Celery Cabbage And
Dried Shrimp Soup

This is a quick, easy, and delicious soup. It must be made, though, with dried shrimp, which have a far more distinctive flavor than the fresh ones.

½ cup dried shrimp
½ cup dry sherry
1 small head celery cabbage
2 tablespoons peanut oil
3 slices fresh ginger root

1½ teaspoons salt
2 cups Basic Chicken Broth
   (see recipe on page 43)
4 cups water

Soak the shrimp in sherry for 30 minutes. Cut the cabbage into 1-inch chunks. Heat the wok. Add the oil and heat until hot. Stir in the cabbage and ginger root. When the cabbage begins to wilt, stir in the salt. Add Chicken Broth, water, shrimp and sherry. Continue simmering until cabbage is translucent.

Basic Chicken Broth

This recipe makes 8 cups of broth.

Neck, back, wingtips, and all
    giblets except the liver of a
    small chicken
Pork bones with meat attached
    (optional if available)

Leftover meat (optional)
1 scallion, tied in a knot
3 slices fresh ginger root
8 cups cold water
Salt to taste

Place the chicken pieces and pork bones along with any leftover meat in the wok. Add the scallion and ginger root. Cover with water. Allow the water to come to a full boil and then reduce the heat to a simmer. Do not allow the developing stock to regain the boil or it will become cloudy. Skim the stock from time to time. Simmer about 30 minutes. Add salt. Strain the stock and shred the meat.

Velvet Corn Soup

1 can (16 ounces) cream-style corn
1 cup Basic Chicken Broth (see
   recipe on page 43)
3 tablespoons dry sherry
Salt

1 tablespoon sugar
1 tablespoon cornstarch combined
   with 2 tablespoons cold water
2 tablespoons finely minced
   Smithfield ham

Place the corn and Chicken Broth in the wok and heat until boiling. Add the sherry and a pinch of salt to taste. Add the sugar. Reduce the heat and simmer for another 2-3 minutes. The soup should be very thick, like a creamy pudding. Add the cornstarch paste a little at a time, continuing to beat and stir, until the right consistency is reached. Garnish each bowl with a little minced ham.

Soup With Shrimp Dumplings

Delicate flavors in a beautifully light soup.

½ pound fresh or dried shrimp,
   minced
⅓ cup ham, minced
1 scallion, minced
½ teaspoon salt
½ teaspoon sugar

2 egg whites, unbeaten
1 tablespoon soy sauce
1 tablespoon cornstarch
4 cups water
6 cups Basic Chicken Broth (see
   recipe on page 43)

On a chopping board, form the shrimp, ham, and scallion into a flat cake. Make a depression in the center of the cake and add to it the salt, sugar, egg whites, soy sauce, and cornstarch. With a cleaver, mince the whole cake, turning with the flat of the blade to make a finely minced mixture. Place in a bowl. Put the water into the wok and bring to a boil. Drop the shrimp mixture in the boiling water about 1 teaspoon at a time. Allow the water to regain the boil. Simmer until the dumplings are pale in color and bubbling to the top. Lift out the dumplings with a slotted spoon and continue cooking the remaining shrimp mixture until it is all used. Serve the dumplings in hot chicken broth. This recipe makes 20 dumplings.

Noodle Soup

Not like Mama used to make.

2 tablespoons peanut oil
½ pound pork, shredded
1 leek, shredded
½ pound spinach, washed and
    shredded
2 quarts water
2 cups Basic Chicken Broth (see
    recipe on page 43) or chicken
    stock
3 tablespoons soy sauce
1 tablespoon sherry
1 teaspoon salt
1 recipe noodles (see recipe on
    page 49), boiled 1 minute,
    then drained
1 egg, beaten (optional)

Heat the wok and add the peanut oil. Stir in the pork, and continue stirring until the color begins to change. Stir in the leek and spinach. Stir to coat with oil, then add the water, Chicken Broth, soy sauce, sherry, and salt. Bring to a boil. (If your wok won't hold all this, transfer to a big kettle.) Add the noodles. Let broth boil again. If you wish to add the egg, add it slowly while stirring. Serve hot.

Watercress Soup For Four

Easiest soup of all.

4 cups Basic Chicken Broth (see recipe on page 43)
½ cup cooked chicken, shredded

1 cup fresh watercress, washed and chopped
Salt

Heat the Chicken Broth in the wok. When it is boiling, stir in the chicken and watercress. Simmer until watercress is just wilted. Add salt to taste. Serve hot.

Noodles

2 cups unsifted flour
1 egg beaten with ⅓ cup cold
    water

Cornstarch

Place flour on a board. Make a well in the flour and add the egg and water mixture. Knead to mix. The dough will be stiff. Knead for about 5 minutes, cover the dough with a damp cloth and let set for ½ hour. Roll the dough into a cylinder and cut into 4 parts. Flour a board heavily with cornstarch. Pat ¼ of the dough into a flat cake, roll the cake very thin, then roll it around the rolling pin, making sure that it is well floured. Roll heavily and evenly. Unroll and reroll until the dough is very thin. Flour on both sides and lay it on the board in accordion pleats. Shred into very thin, even strips. Fluff noodles with both hands, as if fluffing a pillow. Repeat with remaining dough.

To cook noodles: Boil the noodles for 8 minutes in water to cover. Rinse in cold water. Drain.

Soft-Fried Noodles: Heat wok. Add 3 tablespoons oil. When the oil is hot, add cooked noodles (see recipe above) and lower heat. Turn the mass of noodles from time to time until *lightly* browned.

Wontons

Make noodle dough (see recipe page 49), but instead of cutting into noodles, cut into 3-inch squares. Dust squares with flour and set aside.

WONTON FILLING:

½ pound raw meat, ground
2 scallions (white only), minced
1 teaspoon cornstarch
3 teaspoons soy sauce
2 teaspoons wine

Mix all ingredients together and knead to mix well.

To make wontons: Place a small ball of filling just off-center of each square. Moisten the edges with water, fold over, and seal.

To cook: Boil enough water (about 3 cups) to cover the wontons. When it is boiling, drop in the wontons. When it boils again, add 1 cup of cold water; and when it comes to a boil, drain the wontons. Serve in bowls of hot soup or chicken broth.

Deep-Fried Wontons: These wontons may also be deep-fried and dipped in coarse salt for an hors d'oeuvre.

Wonton Soup: Float 3-4 cooked wontons for each person in chicken broth (see recipe, page 43) and garnish with a few tablespoons shredded boktsoi tops or spinach.

Basic Rice

Allow ½ cup rice per person. Put the rice in a heavy pan and wash with cold water if you like. (Washing is necessary to remove the excess starch from white rice, but not so with brown.) Shake the rice to distribute it evenly on the bottom of the pan. Place your index finger gently on top of the rice, being careful not to make a depression. Add water to the depth of the first knuckle—about 1 inch. Place the pan over high heat until it comes to a rolling boil, then cover the pan and turn the heat down to the lowest simmer. White rice will be done in 10-12 minutes —brown in about 25 minutes. The rice is done when little holes appear in the surface and it appears to have risen slightly. If you are not ready to eat, keep the rice over the lowest possible heat rather than turn it off.

Three-Precious Fried Rice

3 tablespoons peanut oil
1 teaspoon salt
½ cup cooked lobster or shrimp
in ¼-inch dice
½ cup cooked pork in ¼-inch dice
½ cup cooked duck or chicken in
¼-inch dice
1 large onion, finely diced
1 large stalk celery, finely diced

1 tablespoon pimiento, minced
2 eggs, lightly beaten
½ cup bean sprouts
½ cup cooked peas, fresh or frozen
6 cups cold, cooked rice
4 tablespoons soy sauce, or to
taste
2 tablespoons minced Chinese
chives or green scallion

Heat the wok. Add the oil. When the oil is hot, add the salt and stir in the lobster, pork, duck, onion, and celery. Stir vigorously until the onion is just transparent. Stir in the pimiento, just to mix, then add the eggs, stirring constantly. Add the bean sprouts and peas. Stir to mix well. Stir in the rice and continue stirring until the rice is thoroughly mixed with the other ingredients. Add the soy sauce, a little at a time, stirring after each addition. The soy sauce will give the rice a lovely light brown color. (Add more soy sauce if it is not salty enough, but more than 6 tablespoons of soy sauce will make most rice too soggy.) Stir in the minced chive or scallion. Serve hot.

Fried Rice With Oyster Sauce

2 tablespoons peanut oil
1 cup cooked, leftover pork, diced
2-3 scallions, diced

3 cups cold cooked rice
1½-2 tablespoons oyster sauce
2 eggs

Heat the peanut oil. Stir in the pork and scallions. Stir in the rice and continue cooking for 2-3 minutes. Add the oyster sauce. Add the eggs one at a time and stir until the eggs begin to set. The rice will be very soft. If you would like a firmer texture, stir the eggs into the pork and scallions before adding the rice.

Spring Rolls

These are called Egg Rolls only in America.

Filling for Spring Roll Skins (see recipe page 55).

8-10 Chinese black dried mushrooms, soaked and minced
1 tablespoon peanut oil
1 cup raw shrimp, minced
3 tablespoons minced raw meat
3 medium celery stalks, minced

1 medium onion, minced
1½ teaspoon salt (or to taste)
1 tablespoon cornstarch combined
with 2 tablespoons cold water
½ cup bean sprouts (optional)

Soak the mushrooms for 20 minutes in a small bowl of warm water. Reserve ⅔ cup of liquid. Heat the oil. Mix together the shrimp, meat, celery, mushrooms, and onion. Stir into the oil until the celery begins to become translucent. Add the salt and stir. Add the reserved liquid and enough cornstarch paste to make it very thick. Remove from heat. Taste for salt—it should be a *little* salty to compensate for the skins. Stir in the sprouts. Place some of the filling diagonally across the bottom of a skin. Fold the bottom corner up and over the filling. Fold the side corners in toward the center. Roll up and seal the remaining flap with some cornstarch paste. Continue similarly until you are out of filling. Cook the rolls by deep-frying until golden and crisp. Serve hot with fresh mustard, and plum sauce.

Spring Roll Skins

1 cup cake flour
1 cup all-purpose flour

1 cup boiling water

Mix the flours together (do not sift) and add the boiling water. Stir with a fork to form a ball. Knead until smooth. Place in a bowl, cover with a damp cloth, and let rest at least 15 minutes. Roll out on a **very** well-floured board (this is a soft, sticky dough) and trim into 5- or 6-inch squares. Flour the squares very well and set aside. Continue until all the dough is used. If the trimmings are sticky enough, they may be kneaded into a ball and re-rolled.

For shu mai, cut into 3- or 4-inch squares.

Shu Mai—Filling

½ cup raw shrimp, shelled and
  deveined
½ cup celery cabbage
¼ cup minced meat
2 scallions (white only)

½ teaspoon salt
½ teaspoon sherry
½ teaspoon fresh ginger root,
  grated

Mince together the shrimp, celery cabbage, meat, and scallions. Add the salt, sherry, and ginger root and mix well. Place a small ball of the filling in the center of a prepared shu mai (spring roll) or wonton skin. Draw up the edges to form a small pouch. Continue until all the filling is used. Place finished shu mai on small squares of waxed paper and steam 20 minutes. Serve hot. (Shu Mai may be garnished with minced ham, parsley, or finely chopped egg.)

Pearl Balls

The glutinous rice, steamed, looks like pearls.

½ cup glutinous rice
1 cup water
1 pound beef, ground
1 egg, beaten
1 tablespoon soy sauce

1 teaspoon salt
1 teaspoon fresh ginger root,
    grated
4 water chestnuts, minced
2 scallions, minced

Cover the rice with water and let it stand for 2 hours. Drain very well and spread rice on a linen towel. Mix the meat with all the other ingredients except the rice. Combine thoroughly. Form walnut-sized balls of the meat mixture. Roll each ball in the rice, pressing to make the grains adhere. Place the riced balls on waxed paper. Place the riced balls on plates or in bowls and steam 30 minutes. Serve hot. Tiny pearl balls could be used as hors d'oeuvres or cocktail nibbles.

Ground Meat Chow Mein

2 tablespoons peanut oil
2 cloves garlic, crushed
½ pound ground beef
6-8 leaves Chinese cabbage, shredded
2 stalks celery, shredded
1 medium onion, shredded
½ cup bamboo shoots, shredded
4-6 Chinese black dried mushrooms, soaked to soften and shredded

2 cups chicken stock
3 tablespoons soy sauce
½ teaspoon sugar
2 tablespoons cornstarch combined with 3 tablespoons cold water
1 recipe Soft-Fried Noodles (see recipe on page 49)
1 tablespoon sesame oil (optional)

Heat the wok. Add the oil. Brown the garlic in oil and discard. Crumble the ground beef into the oil. As the color begins to change, add the cabbage, celery, onion, and bamboo shoots. When the onion is becoming translucent, stir in the mushrooms, stock, soy sauce, and sugar. Simmer 3-4 minutes. Thicken with the cornstarch paste. Pour over the Soft-Fried Noodles. Garnish with sesame oil if desired.

Northern-Style Beef Stew

Marinade:

3 tablespoons soy sauce
½ teaspoon Tabasco sauce
1 tablespoon honey
½ teaspoon five-spice powder
1 teaspoon garlic, minced
2 tablespoons sherry

2 pounds beef, cubed
3-5 cups chicken stock or water
1 medium turnip, sliced (potato
     may be substituted)

Mix together ingredients for the marinade in a bowl. Cover the bowl. Marinate the beef in refrigerator for 12-24 hours. Put the beef and 1 cup stock into the wok. Bring to a boil, cover, and simmer over lowest heat 1½ hours. Add additional stock as needed. Meat should be almost tender. Add turnip and simmer 20 minutes more.

Beef Shreds With Chili Peppers

In Szechuan, hot pepper is the favorite seasoning.

½ pound beef, shredded
2 tablespoons soy sauce
2 tablespoons sherry
1 teaspoon ginger juice*
1½ teaspoons garlic powder or 2
    cloves garlic, crushed

3 tablespoons peanut oil
1 cucumber, seeded and shredded
2 chili peppers, seeded and
    shredded
1 tablespoon cornstarch combined
    with 2 tablespoons cold water

Marinate the beef in a mixture of soy sauce, sherry, ginger juice, and garlic powder for 15 minutes. Remove the beef from the seasonings, reserving the small amount of liquid. Heat the wok. Add the peanut oil and when the oil is very hot, add the beef. Stir the beef until it browns and add the cucumber and chili peppers, stirring rapidly. Add reserved liquid from the beef marinade. Thicken with cornstarch paste.

*Ginger juice is made by squeezing freshly grated ginger through a cheesecloth. I am lazy and usually just use an equal amount of grated ginger.

Sesame Beef

A variation of Dry-Fried Beef.

½ pound flank steak, sliced thinly
Marinade:
3 tablespoons soy sauce
1 tablespoon sesame oil
1 tablespoon honey
1 leek or 1 tablespoon dried leek
½ teaspoon red pepper or ½
   teaspoon Tabasco sauce
1 clove garlic, crushed

1 cup snow peas or thinly sliced
   bamboo shoots
½ cup Basic Chicken Broth
   (see recipe on page 43)
1 tablespoon cornstarch combined
   with 2 tablespoons cold water
1-2 tablespoons white sesame
   seeds for garnish

Marinate the beef in the combined marinade ingredients for 20 minutes. Heat the wok until it is very hot. Do not add any oil. Drain the beef, reserving the marinade. Toss the beef into the hot wok and stir rapidly until it just begins to change color. Stir in the snow peas or bamboo shoots. Add the reserved marinade and the chicken broth. Stir lightly until it comes to a boil. Thicken the liquid with the cornstarch paste, adding a little at a time. Garnish with the sesame seeds.

Dry-Fried Beef

Fragrant and very flavorful.

1 cup sliced beef
3 tablespoons soy sauce
1 tablespoon sesame oil
1 tablespoon honey

1 leek or 2 scallions, shredded
½ teaspoon Tabasco sauce
1 clove garlic, crushed

Mix all of the ingredients. Let stand at least 20 minutes. Heat the wok until it is very hot and add the beef. Stir-fry for 6 minutes or until the beef is tender. No other oil is needed.

Beef With Bok Choy

Marinade:

1 tablespoon cornstarch
3 tablespoons soy sauce
½ teaspoon sugar
½ teaspoon fresh ginger root, grated
½ pound flank or round steak, sliced very thinly

4 or 5 stalks bok choy
3 tablespoons peanut oil
2 cloves garlic, crushed
½ teaspoon salt
½ cup water

Mix together the cornstarch, soy sauce, sugar, and ginger root. Add the beef, and let stand 20 minutes in marinade. Separate the white stalks of the bok choy from the leaves. Cut the stalks into 2-inch-long sections and shred about ⅓-inch wide. Shred the leaves. Heat the wok. Heat the peanut oil. Add the garlic. Discard the garlic when it is browned. Add the salt. Stir in the beef, reserving the marinade. Stir the beef until the color begins to change. Add the bok choy stalks and stir until they begin to become translucent. Add the leaves, then add the marinade and the water. Stir until the sauce boils and is smooth. Serve immediately.

CHINESE BEEF WITH SNOW PEAS: Using the above recipe, omit the bok choy and substitute ½-¾ pound fresh snow peas. Drop the snow peas in boiling water just until their color brightens. Rinse with cold water. Add to the cooking beef as you would the bok choy stalks.

Beef With Oyster Sauce

One of the happiest combinations.

Marinade:

3 tablespoons oyster sauce
1 tablespoon soy sauce
¼ teaspoon salt
1 tablespoon wine
1 teaspoon sugar
1 teaspoon fresh ginger root,
   grated
1 tablespoon cornstarch

½ pound steak, sliced very thin
2 tablespoons peanut oil
1 large onion, sliced thick
3 stalks bok choy, whites sliced
   thin, greens shredded
½ cup chicken stock

Mix the marinade ingredients and toss with the meat. Let stand 15-20 minutes. Heat the wok. Add the peanut oil. When the oil is hot, drain the meat, reserving the marinade and stir the meat in the hot oil, just enough to coat with oil. Immediately stir in the onions and whites of bok choy. Stir until the onions begin to become translucent. Stir in the bok choy greens. Mix the reserved marinade with the stock and add to the meat. Stir until it reaches a boil and is slightly thick. Serve hot.

Beef Liver With Ginger And Bean Sprouts

½-¾ pound beef liver
2 teaspoons fresh ginger root, shredded
2 tablespoons sherry
½ teaspoon salt
4 tablespoons peanut oil
2 large onions, sliced thinly
1 cup fresh bean sprouts
½ teaspoon sugar
2 tablespoons soy sauce

Cut the liver into ½-inch pieces. Toss in a small bowl with the ginger root, sherry, and salt. Let stand for 20 minutes. Heat the wok. Heat 3 tablespoons of the peanut oil and stir in the liver. Stir over high heat until browned and slightly crisp. Remove the liver from the wok and keep warm in 300° oven. Add remaining peanut oil if needed. Stir in the onions and cook until translucent. Stir in the bean sprouts, sugar, and soy sauce. Stir in the liver and cook over high heat until liver is very hot. The sherry and ginger root combine to give the liver a mild, delicate flavor.

Curry Pork Noodles

A favorite in a popular Chinese restaurant.

1 cup pork, shredded
2 tablespoons sherry combined
    with 2 teaspoons cornstarch
2 tablespoons peanut oil
2 cloves garlic, crushed
1 tablespoon curry powder
1 large onion, sliced

2 medium tomatoes, peeled,
    seeded, and sliced
1 cup Basic Chicken Broth (see
    recipe on page 43)
Salt to taste
1 recipe Soft-Fried Noodles (see
    recipe on page 49)

Mix the pork with sherry and cornstarch. Marinate for 20 minutes. Heat the wok. Heat the peanut oil, brown and discard the garlic.

Stir in the curry powder, onion, and pork. When the pork is tender, after about 5 minutes, stir in tomatoes, chicken broth, and any remaining pork marinade. Season to taste with salt. Heat to boiling point and pour over noodles. Toss and serve.

Szechuanese Twice-Cooked Pork

You could use leftover pork, too.

2 pounds lean pork with bone
2 tablespoons peanut oil
1 clove garlic, crushed
1 scallion cut into 1-inch pieces
    and shredded
2 tablespoons hoi sin sauce

1 teaspoon fresh ginger root,
    grated
1 teaspoon sugar
½ teaspoon Tabasco sauce
½ cup Basic Chicken Broth
    (see recipe on page 43)
½ cup bean sprouts

Place the pork in the wok. Cover with water and simmer, covered, for 1 hour. Remove the pork from the water and allow to cool. Remove the bone from the pork and slice pork across the grain into ¼-inch slices. Heat the wok. Heat the peanut oil. Add the garlic. Brown and then discard the garlic. Stir in the pork. Stir in the scallion, hoi sin sauce, ginger root, sugar, and Tabasco sauce. Add the Basic Chicken Broth and stir until blended. Stir in the bean sprouts and continue stirring until the sprouts have wilted slightly. Serve hot.

Water Chestnuts With Minced Meat (Mah Tuy Soong)

2 tablespoons peanut oil
½ cup pork, minced
1 cup fresh water chestnuts, minced
½ teaspoon salt
1 teaspoon soy sauce

Dash black pepper
1 cup Basic Chicken Broth (see recipe on page 43)
1 tablespoon cornstarch combined with 2 tablespoons cold water
Leaves of 1 head of Boston lettuce

Heat the wok; add the peanut oil and heat. Add the pork, water, chestnuts, salt, soy sauce, and pepper. Stir over high heat for 1 minute. Add the Chicken Broth; cover and cook for 2 minutes. Add the cornstarch paste gradually. Toss until thickened. Serve the pork mixture in a bowl. The diner places about 2 tablespoons of the mixture on a lettuce leaf and eats it with his fingers. This dish is an exaltation of fresh water chestnuts—made with canned water chestnuts, it is very flat.

Red Stewed Pork Or Beef

The Chinese prefer to cook the pork with the fat left on. We remove it. If you decide to retain the fat, increase the first 2 hours of cooking time by 1 hour.

If you buy a 6-pound pork shoulder, 2 pounds of the lean pork may be removed and used for another dish such as pineapple pork and the remaining 4 pounds can be red-stewed.

4 pounds pork shoulder, fresh
   ham, shin of beef, or chuck
   roast with bone
½ cup soy sauce
4 slices fresh ginger root

3 scallions, knotted
¼ cup sherry
2 cups cold water
1 tablespoon brown sugar

Place all of the ingredients except the brown sugar in the wok. Bring to a simmer, cover, and simmer for 2 hours, turning the meat at the end of the first hour. Add the sugar and cook ½ hour longer. The meat should be easy to pierce with a chopstick. Remove the scallions and ginger root. Serve with only a little of the cooking liquid. Reserve the remaining liquid for adding to other dishes. This liquid is a master sauce and gives a beautiful flavor to many other preparations.

VARIATIONS: For Red Stewed Beef, add 2 cloves star anise. Add 2 cups diced turnip or potato the last 20 minutes of cooking.

Pineapple Pork With Ginger And Leeks

½ pound lean pork, sliced thin
1 tablespoon soy sauce
1 tablespoon sherry
1 tablespoon cornstarch
1 14-ounce can pineapple chunks
2 tablespoons peanut oil

1 clove garlic, crushed
1 small onion, cut into chunks
2 leeks: split into half lengthwise
    and sliced into 1-inch sections
1 tablespoon fresh ginger root,
    shredded

Mix the pork with the soy sauce, sherry, and cornstarch. Let stand for 10 minutes. Drain the pineapple, reserving the juice. Heat the wok. Add the peanut oil, then the garlic. Brown and discard the garlic. Drain and add the pork, reserving marinating liquid. When the pork appears white in color, add onion, leeks, and ginger root. Stir until onion appears translucent. Stir in reserved pork marinade and pineapple juice. Let liquid come to a boil. Stir in pineapple chunks. Thin liquid with a little water if it appears too thick.

Spareribs With Pineapple

2 pounds spareribs
½ cup soy sauce
¼ cup brown sugar
¼ cup cider vinegar
1 clove garlic, crushed
½ cup water

1 14-ounce can pineapple chunks
2 tablespoons peanut oil
1 tablespoon flour
½ teaspoon salt
1 tablespoon cornstarch combined
    with 2 tablespoons cold water

Cut the spareribs across the bone into 3-inch sections. Separate the ribs. Marinate in soy sauce for 30 minutes. Drain. Combine the sugar, vinegar, garlic, and water. Add juice from the canned pineapple. Heat the wok. Heat the peanut oil, stir in the ribs and cook until brown. Stir in the flour. Stir in the juice mixture. Cover and simmer for 1 hour. Add the salt and cornstarch paste and heat. Stir in pineapple chunks. Serve hot.

Note: This recipe may be prepared ahead, but add the pineapple chunks at the last minute.

Steamed Spareribs
With Black Beans

1 pound spareribs
2 quarts boiling water
¼ cup black beans (fermented
    black beans—dow see)
2 stalks scallion
4 cloves garlic

1 teaspoon salt
1 tablespoon sesame oil
2 teaspoons cornstarch
2 tablespoons water
2 tablespoons sherry

Cut the spareribs into 2-inch long pieces. Drop the ribs into the 2 quarts boiling water. Remove after 5 minutes and drain. Place the beans in a bowl that will fit in your steamer. Mash them with the handle of a cleaver. Mince the scallion and add to the beans. Add the garlic by pressing through a garlic press. Add the salt, sesame oil, cornstarch, 2 tablespoons water, and sherry. Stir to mix well. Add ribs and toss to coat with bean mixture. Place bowl with ribs and bean mixture in steamer and steam 30-40 minutes or until the ribs are tender.

Chicken And Rice Japanese Style

Quick to make!

½ cup sake
2 tablespoons mirin (sweetened
    sake) (2 tablespoons sugar
    may be substituted)
5 tablespoons soy sauce
1 tablespoon sugar
½ cup chicken stock
⅛ teaspoon salt

1 pair chicken breasts, diced
½ cup frozen peas
2 medium onions, sliced thinly
6 eggs, beaten
6 bowls hot, cooked rice
1 square nori seaweed passed over
    a flame to crisp

Heat the sake, mirin, soy sauce, sugar, stock, and salt in a wok. Add the chicken, peas, and onions. Cook over a medium heat until the chicken is cooked. Remove the wok from the heat and stir in the eggs. In Japanese cooking, the eggs should not be quite set. If you wish firmer eggs, return the wok to the heat and stir a few times until the right consistency is achieved. Top each bowl of rice with some of the chicken-egg mixture. Crumble nori seaweed over the top as a garnish.

White Chicken With Mushrooms (Moo Goo Gai Pan)

1 chicken breast, boned, skinned, and cut in ½-inch cubes
¼ cup wine
Sprinkle of salt
2 stalks celery
1 small onion
14-16 snow peas
4-5 fresh or canned water chestnuts

2 tablespoons peanut oil
½ cup fresh mushrooms, sliced
½ cup water
¾ teaspoon salt
¼ teaspoon sugar
1½ teaspoons cornstarch combined with ¼ cup cold water

Marinate the chicken in wine and salt. Cut the celery in half lengthwise, then cut in quarter-inch cubes. Dice onion. Cut snow peas into thirds. Peel and slice water chestnuts (just slice the canned ones). Heat the peanut oil in a wok. Stir in the chicken, reserving any marinade. Stir in the onion, then the celery. Stir until the chicken begins to turn white. Add the snow peas, mushrooms, and water chestnuts if canned variety is used. Stir the water into the marinade and add to the wok. Add the salt and sugar. Let cook about 5 minutes. Stir in cornstarch paste and cook for a few minutes. Stir in fresh water chestnuts, if canned have not been used. Serve hot. As this is a "white" dish, salt is used, but *no* soy sauce.

Iri-Dori

This is a very distinctive Japanese chicken stew.

4-5 Chinese black dried
    mushrooms (optional)
1 tablespoon peanut oil
1 whole large chicken breast cut
    into ½-inch pieces, diced
1 large carrot, diced
1 leek or 1 small onion cut into
    ½-inch slices
1 medium sweet potato, raw,
    peeled, and diced

1 small can bamboo shoots,
    drained (about ½ cup)
½ cup Basic Chicken Broth
    (see recipe on page 43)
¼ cup sherry
3 tablespoons sugar
¼ cup soy sauce
½ cup fresh or frozen green peas
    (parboil if fresh)

Soak the mushrooms for 20 minutes in a small bowl of warm water. Discard the stems and dice the caps. Heat the peanut oil in the wok over high heat. Sauté the chicken, carrot, and leek until chicken turns white. Add the mushrooms, potato, bamboo shoots, chicken broth, sherry, and sugar. Cover and cook over medium heat for 10 minutes, or until potato is tender. Raise the heat. Add the soy sauce. Cook for a few minutes more to reduce the liquid. Stir in the peas. Continue cooking 3 minutes and serve hot.

Chicken Wings In Oyster Sauce

One of those snacks you can't stop eating!

2 pounds chicken wings, disjointed
½ cup peanut oil
3 tablespoons oyster sauce
3 slices fresh ginger root
2½ tablespoons soy sauce

1 teaspoon sugar
1 teaspoon sherry
1 cup Basic Chicken Broth (see
   recipe on page 43)

Use only the second and third joints of the chicken wings for this recipe. The tips of the wings may be reserved for making the chicken broth. Dry the wings. Heat the oil and brown the wings a few at a time. When all the wings have been browned, discard the oil. Return the wings to the wok with all of the remaining ingredients. Bring to a boil. Cover and simmer 10 minutes. Remove the cover and boil lightly 15 minutes until only a small quantity of liquid remains, stirring occasionally. Raise the heat and boil until only about ½ cup liquid remains. Serve hot or cold.

Chicken With Almonds

A medley of texture.

1 pair chicken breasts, sliced
   thinly
1 teaspoon salt
2 tablespoons wine
1 tablespoon cornstarch

About 4 ounces slivered almonds
2 tablespoons peanut oil
1 small onion, sliced
2 ounces snow peas
½ cup chicken stock

Mix the sliced chicken with the salt, wine, and cornstarch. Place the almonds in a cold wok and stir over medium heat until the almonds begin to toast. Remove them from the wok and set aside. Heat the wok. Add the peanut oil and stir in the chicken, reserving any marinade. When chicken begins to turn white, stir in the onion. Stir a few times. Stir in the snow peas, stock, and reserved marinade. Stir 1 to 2 minutes until the onion is translucent and soft. Stir in about ¾ of the almonds. Serve immediately, sprinkled with the remaining almonds.

Variation: For the chicken, substitute ½ pound very thinly sliced lean pork. Stir pork until it is entirely light in color before adding onions.

Lemon Sauce Chicken

Batter:

    1½ cups instantized flour
    1 tablespoon baking powder
    ½ teaspoon salt

    ¼ teaspoon sugar
    ½ cup peanut oil
    1 cup iced water

Oil for deep-frying 2 chicken breasts, skinned, boned and sliced.

Sauce:

    1 cup Basic Chicken Broth (see
      recipe on page 43)
    ¼ cup sherry
    1 tablespoon soy sauce
    1 teaspoon honey or sugar

    3 tablespoons fresh lemon juice
    Grated rind of 1 lemon
    1 tablespoon cornstarch combined
      with 2 tablespoons cold water

Mix the ingredients for the batter in the order listed. Stir to form a smooth batter. Heat the peanut oil in the wok until it reaches 370°. Dip the chicken slices in the batter and deep-fry for 8 minutes until cooked. Drain the chicken and keep hot in a 350° oven. The outside of the chicken will remain crisp. Combine all of the ingredients for the sauce except the cornstarch paste. Heat the sauce ingredients to boiling. Add the cornstarch paste a little at a time, stirring until desired consistency is reached. Pour the sauce over the chicken and garnish with lemon slices. The deep-fried chicken may be served without sauce as an hors d'oeuvre.

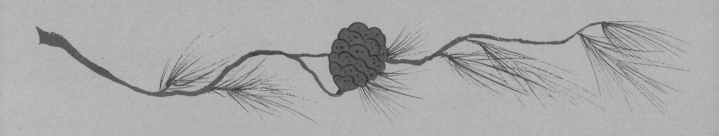

Empress Chicken (Red Stewed)

Wings and legs of 1 chicken
1 cup bamboo shoots
2 slices fresh ginger root
1 tablespoon sherry
1 scallion, knotted

½ teaspoon salt
4 cloves star anise (optional)
2 cups Basic Chicken Broth (see recipe on page 43)
6 tablespoons soy sauce

Cut the chicken wings and legs into 1½-inch chunks through the bone. Cut bamboo shoots into slices. Combine all of the ingredients in the wok and heat to boiling. Reduce heat, cover, and simmer until almost tender, about ½ hour. Remove lid and simmer another 10 minutes to reduce liquid. Remove ginger and scallion before serving. This dish may be prepared in advance and reheated.

Chicken Wings Stuffed With Smithfield Ham

A banquet dish fit for an emperor.

1 pound chicken wings
1½ cups water
1 slice Smithfield ham (about ¼ pound) cut into thin strips

½ teaspoon salt
2 tablespoons sherry
1 tablespoon cornstarch combined with ¼ cup cold water

Wash the wings and cut each wing into three sections, being careful to cut at the joint. Discard the tips or save for stock. Place wings in the wok and add the water. Bring to a boil. Place lid on the wok and simmer for 1 hour. Remove the wings from the broth and allow them to cool. Slip the bones from the remaining sections and fill each cavity with a strip of ham. Measure the cooking liquid. If there is less than 1 cup, add enough water to make one cup. If there is more, allow it to boil down to one cup. Add the salt and sherry. Place over moderate heat and allow to boil. Stir in the cornstarch paste. Heat wings in the sauce. This dish may be prepared ahead and reheated.

Sweet And Sour Chicken

Colorful and delicious.

1 tablespoon peanut oil
½ teaspoon salt
1 pair chicken breasts, diced
1 large onion, in chunks
1 green pepper, cut in 1-inch
    cubes

1 large tomato, peeled, seeded,
    and cut in 1-inch cubes
1 recipe Sweet and Sour Sauce
    (see recipe on page 120)

Heat the wok. Add the peanut oil and salt. Add the chicken, onion, and pepper, and stir vigorously until chicken is white. Add the tomato and stir gently for 1 minute, or until heated. Add the Sweet and Sour Sauce. Serve hot.

VARIATIONS: This dish may be made with pork instead of chicken. Shrimp could be used, too, but is not as good.

Green Pepper Chicken

1 teaspoon cornstarch
2 teaspoons sherry
Pinch salt
1 cup white chicken meat, diced
2 green peppers, diced
2 tablespoons peanut oil

1 bamboo shoot, diced
3 water chestnuts, diced
1 tablespoon soy sauce
2-3 tablespoons Basic Chicken
  Broth or water (see recipe on
  page 43)

Combine the cornstarch, sherry, and salt and mix well with the diced chicken. Allow the chicken to stand for 20 minutes. Parboil the green peppers for 6 minutes. Drain. Heat the wok. Add the peanut oil. Stir in the chicken and continue stirring until the chicken turns white. Add the peppers and all of the remaining ingredients. Stir for 1 minute, until all the ingredients are hot.

Crispy Spiced Duck

An easy version of a complicated classic.

1 duckling, about 4 pounds
2 tablespoons fresh ginger root, minced
⅛ teaspoon dry mustard
⅛ teaspoon black pepper
⅛ teaspoon five-spice powder
2 teaspoons salt
1 tablespoon soy sauce

2 tablespoons cornstarch
½ teaspoon molasses
2 teaspoons wine
Oil for deep-frying
2 tablespoons cornstarch combined with 3 tablespoons cold water (optional)
Hoi sin sauce

Quarter the duckling. Mix together the ginger root, mustard, black pepper, five-spice powder, and salt. Rub the mixture over the duckling and let it stand for 1 hour. Place the pieces of duckling in bowls and cover with foil. Steam for 2 hours. It may be necessary to use 2 bowls and a 2-tiered steamer. Remove the bowls from the steamer. Remove the duckling from the bowls and when it is cool enough to handle, rub each piece with a mixture of soy sauce, cornstarch, molasses, and wine. Heat oil to 350° and fry the duckling, one piece at a time, until brown and crispy. Keep in a warm oven, 300° (up to ½ hour). Serve on a bed of Stirred Lettuce (see recipe on page 101) with hoi sin sauce as a dip. If you want to make a sauce of the duckling's steaming liquid from the bowls, pour it into a saucepan and thicken it with the cornstarch paste. Serve it separately, or on the lettuce, but *not* on the duckling, as it would diminish the crispness.

Fish Puffs

Something better than plain fresh fish.

1 pound fish fillets, minced or
    ground
1 teaspoon fresh ginger root,
    grated
1 scallion, minced

1 egg
1 tablespoon sherry
½ teaspoon salt
1 teaspoon cornstarch
Peanut oil for deep-frying

Combine all of the ingredients and form the fish mixture into walnut-sized balls. Deep fry the fish balls for 3 to 5 minutes in the peanut oil heated to 370°. Serve with a sweet and sour sauce or on a bed of stirred bok choy or spinach.

Steamed Fish

One of the best fish recipes from a nation of fish fanciers.

1 fresh fish weighing about 1½ pounds (Any nonoily white fish will do, but sea bass is best. Please leave the head and tail in place!)
1 teaspoon fresh ginger root, grated

1½ teaspoons salt
1 tablespoon sherry
1 whole leek, shredded
1 cup boiling water
1 tablespoon peanut oil
1 clove garlic
2 teaspoons sesame oil

Place the fish on a dish that is large enough to both hold it on the steamer and allow the steam to circulate around it. If necessary bend the fish a little. Mix the ginger root and salt together and rub on the fish. The fish should be scored lightly to allow the flavoring to penetrate through the flesh. Sprinkle the sherry and shredded leek over the fish. Place 1 cup boiling water in the wok. Place the fish plate on the steamer and steam for 20 minutes or until the flesh is opaque. Heat the peanut oil. Brown and discard the garlic. Add the sesame oil and allow it to become warm, but not too hot. Pour the oil mixture over the fish and serve.

Variations: Add 1 tablespoon crushed black beans and 1 clove garlic, crushed, into the ginger root and salt combination.

For the ginger root, substitute 3 to 4 tablespoons Chinese mixed sweet ginger pickles, shredded. Add with the leek.

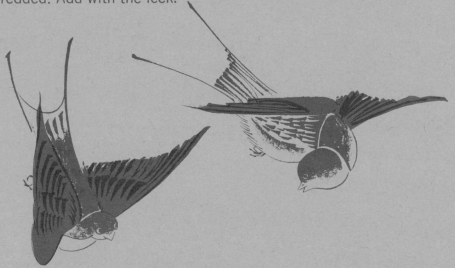

Shrimp With Lobster Sauce

Flavorings:

    3 cloves garlic, crushed

    1 teaspoon fresh ginger root, grated

    1 tablespoon fermented black beans, washed and crushed

Stock Mixture:

    1 cup Basic Chicken Broth or water (see recipe on page 43)

    1 teaspoon sugar

    1 teaspoon soy sauce

    2 tablespoons sherry

    1 teaspoon salt

    3 scallions (white only), minced

    2 tablespoons peanut oil

    3-4 tablespoons raw pork, minced (equivalent of 1 small pork chop)

    1 pound raw shrimp, shelled and deveined (cut into bite-sized pieces)

Thickenings:

    1 tablespoon cornstarch combined with 2 tablespoons cold water

    1 egg, lightly beaten

Garnish:

    3 scallions (green only), minced

Combine the flavorings, crushing them lightly with a spoon. Combine the chicken broth, sugar, soy sauce, sherry, salt, and white of scallions. Heat the wok and add the peanut oil. When the oil is hot, stir in the pork and continue cooking until the pork turns white. Stir in the shrimp, tossing them for a few seconds to coat with oil. Add the flavoring mixture. Stir well. Add the stock mixture and cook until the shrimp turns pink, about 2 minutes. Add the cornstarch paste. Stir until thickened. Remove the wok from the heat and stir in the beaten egg. Serve dish garnished with green scallion. The sauce is delicious on rice.

Note: This dish is very quickly prepared and should be made after the diners are seated, as it must be served immediately. The sauce is the same as that used for Lobster Cantonese and this is how the name of this dish is derived.

Variation: Omit black beans.

Shrimp Kair-Tsup

The Chinese claim that Kair-tsup was invented by the Chinese who cooked for the workers who built the American railroads.

1 tablespoon peanut oil
2 cloves garlic, crushed
½ teaspoon salt
1 pound raw shrimp, shelled and deveined
2 small zucchinis or 1 small fuzzy melon, scraped and sliced
1 tablespoon soy sauce

1 teaspoon grated fresh ginger root
3 tablespoons ketchup
1 teaspoon hoisin sauce (optional)
2 tablespoons sherry
½ cup chicken stock
1 tablespoon cornstarch, combined with 2 tablespoons cold water (optional)

Heat the wok. Add the peanut oil. Fry the garlic in the oil until it is brown, then discard it. Add the salt. Stir in the shrimp and zucchini and stir until shrimp begins to be opaque. Add the soy sauce, ginger root, ketchup, hoi sin sauce, sherry, and stock and stir until shrimp is done. Thicken with cornstarch paste if desired.

Plain Stir-Fried Shrimp

Simple and attractive.

2 tablespoons sherry
2 teaspoons cornstarch
1 teaspoon salt
2 tablespoons peanut oil
4 slices fresh ginger root,
    smashed with flat blade of
    cleaver

1 pound raw shrimp, shelled and
    deveined
1 small onion, sliced
1 scallion (white and green
    minced separately)

Combine the sherry, cornstarch, and salt. Heat the wok. Add the peanut oil and heat until very hot. Add the ginger root and remove when it has browned. Add the shrimp, onion, and white part of the scallion. Stir another 3-5 minutes until the shrimp is just opaque—the timing will depend on the size of the shrimp. Add the sherry mixture and stir only until thickened. Serve hot, garnished with minced green part of the scallion.

Snow Peas With Water Chestnuts

A different vegetable dish for an American meal.

1½ **pounds fresh snow peas**	1½ **cups water**
1 **small can water chestnuts**	½ **teaspoon salt**
½ **teaspoon sugar**	

String the peas as you would string beans. Drain the water chestnuts. Add the sugar to 1 cup of the water. Add the water chestnuts and allow them to stand for 10 minutes. Drain and slice the water chestnuts. Bring the remaining ½ cup of water to a boil in the wok. Add the salt to the boiling water. Add the snow peas. Stir and allow the water to regain the boil. Cover and simmer over lowest heat about 12 minutes—the peas should be bright green and barely tender. Add the water chestnuts to the peas. Stir and heat until the water chestnuts are hot. Drain and serve hot.

Stuffed Mushrooms

A large reward for a small effort and very pretty.

8-10 Chinese black dried
    mushrooms
¼ cup shrimp, minced
1-2 scallions (white and green
    minced separately)

1 teaspoon sherry
1 teaspoon soy sauce
1 teaspoon cornstarch
1 egg, beaten
Salt to taste

Soak the mushrooms for 20 minutes in a small bowl of warm water. Remove the stems and discard, leaving caps whole. Combine the shrimp, white part of the scallion, sherry, soy sauce, cornstarch, egg, and salt. Press about 2 teaspoons of this mixture into the mushroom caps. Place on a plate on steamer in wok and steam for 10 minutes, or until the shrimp mixture is firm. Garnish with the green part of the scallion.

Chinese Vegetable Combination

Vegetarian "chop suey."

6-7 Chinese black dried
    mushrooms
2 tablespoons peanut oil
1 clove garlic, crushed
1 small bok choy, sliced thinly
½ teaspoon salt

1 tablespoon bean sauce
    (optional)
2-3 water chestnuts, sliced
1 cup bean sprouts
1 teaspoon cornstarch combined
    with 1 tablespoon cold water
1 tablespoon sesame oil (optional)

Soak the mushrooms for 20 minutes in a small bowl of warm water. Discard the stems and slice the caps and put aside. Reserve ½ cup liquid. Heat the wok. Heat the peanut oil and add the garlic. Discard the garlic when browned. Stir in the white stems of the bok choy, mushrooms, and salt. Stir in the bok choy tops when the white stems appear translucent. Add the mushroom-soaking liquid and optional bean sauce; stir. Finally, add the water chestnuts and bean sprouts. Heat water chestnuts and bean sprouts until hot. Thicken any remaining liquid with the cornstarch paste. Serve hot. Can be garnished with 1 tablespoon sesame oil.

String Beans With Fermented Bean Curd (Fuyu)

A favorite Cantonese method of preparing beans.

1½ cups fresh string beans	½ cup cold water
1 tablespoon fermented bean curd	2 tablespoons peanut oil
¼ teaspoon sugar	¼ teaspoon salt

Wash and string the beans. Break into 2-inch sections. Combine bean curd with sugar and water. Heat the wok. Heat the oil until very hot. Stir in the beans. Add the salt and bean curd mixture. Reduce the heat, cover, and cook 10 minutes until the beans are tender. This recipe can also be used for preparing broccoli flowerets.

Plain Stirred Spinach

Even children like this spinach!

1 tablespoon peanut oil
1 clove garlic, crushed
½ teaspoon salt

1 pound spinach, washed, drained, leaves torn in half

Heat the wok. Add the oil. Drop in the garlic and remove when browned. Add the salt. Add the spinach and stir with a salad-tossing motion. In less than a minute, the spinach will deepen in color and begin to get limp. Remove from the wok and serve immediately.

Plain-Stirred Lettuce: Use the above recipe, substituting a large head of lettuce, washed, drained, and torn.

Seasoned Mushrooms

A tasty snack.

1½ cups Chinese black dried
    mushrooms
1 tablespoon peanut oil
1 teaspoon fresh ginger root,
    minced

2 tablespoons soy sauce or
    oyster sauce
2 teaspoons sugar

Soak the mushrooms in a small bowl of warm water for 20 minutes. Discard the stems and water; cut caps into bite-sized pieces. Heat the wok. Add the peanut oil. Stir in the mushrooms and add ginger root. Stir in the remaining ingredients and continue stirring until they are "absorbed" by the mushrooms. Serve hot or cold. These mushrooms will keep in the refrigerator for a few days.

Stir-Fried Bok Choy

1 medium head bok choy
2 tablespoons peanut oil

1 teaspoon salt
½ teaspoon sugar

Separate the stalks of bok choy and wash carefully. Cut the green leaves away from the white part. Cut the white into 2-inch lengths, then shred to make strips about ⅓-inch wide. Shred the green leaves. Heat the wok. Add the peanut oil. Add the salt. Stir in the white stalks and cook, stirring until they begin to become translucent. Stir in the green leaves until they begin to wilt. Stir in the sugar. Taste, adding salt if necessary. Serve immediately.

Stuffed Fuzzy Melon

1 fuzzy melon
2 squares preserved turnip,
    soaked in warm water for
    20 minutes and minced

2 tablespoons raw meat, minced

Scrape fuzz off the melon and cut in half lengthwise. Remove the seeds and stuff with mixture of turnip and meat. Steam 20 minutes. Serve hot.

Stuffed Cucumber

Filling:

1 plump cucumber
3 tablespoons raw meat, minced
2 canned water chestnuts, minced

1-2 tablespoons bamboo shoots,
  minced
1 teaspoon beaten egg

Sauce:

1 tablespoon peanut oil
1 clove garlic, crushed
½ cup Basic Chicken Broth
  (see recipe on page 43)

½ teaspoon soy sauce
1 teaspoon cornstarch combined
  with 1 tablespoon cold water

Filling: Halve the cucumber lengthwise. Remove the seeds carefully. Do not pierce the ends. Combine the remaining ingredients for the filling in a small bowl. Stuff the cucumber cavity with the filling mixture. Steam 20 minutes. Slice in ½-inch rounds. Serve covered with the sauce.

Sauce: Heat the peanut oil. Brown and discard the garlic. Add the chicken broth and soy sauce. Bring to a boil. Stir in cornstarch paste. Taste the sauce; add salt if necessary.

Stir-Fried Vegetables

A dish to convert all vegetable haters instantly.

7-8 Chinese black dried
     mushrooms, soaked
3 tablespoons peanut oil
1 teaspoon salt
1 small onion cut into small
     chunks
1 stalk of celery, thinly sliced

1 scallion, (white only), coarsely
     chopped
1 cup celery cabbage, coarsely
     chopped
1 cup lettuce, coarsely chopped
½ teaspoon sesame oil

Soak the mushrooms in a small bowl of warm water for 20 minutes. Reserve ½ cup liquid. Discard mushroom stems, slice caps, and put aside. Heat the wok. Heat the peanut oil to smoking point and add the salt. Add the onion and stir briefly. Add the celery and stir once, add the scallion, mushrooms, and celery cabbage. Stir until the cabbage leaves begin to wilt; then add the lettuce and stir just to mix. Add the reserved liquid and let it come to a boil. Simmer for two minutes or until the heavy stalk of the celery cabbage is translucent. Serve hot. Sprinkle with sesame oil just before serving.

VARIATIONS: In place of, or in addition to, celery and onion you may use: sliced leek, snow peas, green pepper, white mushroom slices, bok choy stems, peeled and sliced broccoli stems, Chinese broccoli. Black mushrooms may be omitted and Basic Chicken Broth replaces the mushroom water.

In place of, or in addition to, celery cabbage, and lettuce you may use: shredded spinach, bok choy tops, collard, mustard green, broccoli flowerets.

Chinese Cabbage With Black Dried Mushrooms

8 Chinese black dried mushrooms
2 tablespoons sherry
2 tablespoons peanut oil
1 or 2 cloves garlic, crushed

1 teaspoon salt
1 small head Chinese cabbage,
   coarsely shredded
2 teaspoons sesame oil

Soak the mushrooms for 20 minutes in a small bowl of warm water. Reserve ½ cup of the mushroom water. Remove and discard the stems from the mushrooms and shred the caps. Add the sherry to reserved mushroom water. Heat the wok. Heat the peanut oil until very hot. Add the garlic. Allow the garlic to brown lightly and then discard it. Add the salt to the hot oil and stir in the cabbage. When the cabbage has just begun to wilt, stir in the mushrooms. Add the mushroom water and sherry and continue cooking over a high heat, stirring occasionally until the cabbage just appears translucent. Place the cabbage in a serving dish and sprinkle with the sesame oil.

Variation: Substitute guy choy (Chinese mustard green) for the Chinese cabbage.

Steamed Chinese Cabbage

1 small head Chinese cabbage　　　　**2 tablespoons sherry**
1 teaspoon salt

Shred the cabbage into ½-inch sections. Place in a bowl small enough to fit in the steamer. Place in the wok. Sprinkle with the salt and sherry. Steam for 20 minutes.

Hot Cabbage Salad

2 strips bacon
1 small head cabbage, shredded
    coarsely
¼ cup sherry

2 tablespoons instantized flour
3 tablespoons cider vinegar
2 tablespoons sugar
⅛ teaspoon black pepper

Place the bacon strips along the bottom of the wok. Heat the wok and cook the bacon until crisp, turning several times. Remove and drain the bacon. Add the cabbage to the hot bacon fat in the wok. Toss to coat with fat. Stir in the sherry and continue stirring for 2 minutes. Stir in the flour, vinegar, sugar, and black pepper. Stir until the cabbage is beginning to appear translucent. Transfer cabbage to a serving bowl and garnish with crumbled bacon.

Spiced Eggplant Hors D'Oeuvre

1 medium-sized eggplant, about
   1 pound
2 teaspoons salt
1 cup instantized flour
¼ teaspoon turmeric

1 teaspoon cumin
¼ teaspoon cayenne
Pinch cinnamon
¾ cup cold water
Peanut oil for deep-frying

Cut the eggplant into ½-inch thick slices—do not peel. Cut the slices in half and sprinkle with salt. Let stand about ½ hour. Mix the flour, turmeric, cumin, cayenne, and cinnamon. Stir in the cold water to make a thick paste. Heat the oil in a wok. Squeeze the eggplant slices to remove water and drain on paper towels. When the oil in the wok reaches 350°, dip 5 or 6 slices into the flour mixture, coating them well, then drop them into the hot oil. Let cook until golden, remove from the oil, and drain. Keep fried slices in warm oven (300°) while frying the rest. Serve alone or with chutney.

Egg Pockets

A Chinese version of an omelet.

3 tablespoons peanut oil
½ pound ground meat
1 scallion, minced
Pinch sugar

Scant ½ teaspoon salt
1 teaspoon sesame oil
4 eggs

Heat 1 tablespoon of the peanut oil in the wok. Add the ground meat and stir until almost done. Stir in the scallion, sugar, salt, and sesame oil. Stir until done. Set aside to cool. Beat eggs lightly. Put a very small quantity of the remaining oil in the wok. Add 3 tablespoons egg and allow to "set." It will form a thin curved pancake in the wok. Put 1 tablespoon meat filling on the pancake, just off the center, and fold the egg pocket over. Press the edges together lightly. Turn pancake with a spatula to allow it to brown lightly on the other side. Repeat this process until all of the egg is used. Keep pockets warm in a 300° oven. The wok has a beautifully smooth surface and the egg will not stick to it. Regular pancakes can also be made in a wok using butter and folding them in the usual way!

Savory Custard

The Chinese soufflé.

2 eggs, beaten lightly
3 tablespoons raw beef, minced
1 tablespoon soy sauce
1 teaspoon sherry
1 teaspoon salt

1 cup Basic Chicken Broth
  (see recipe on page 43)
1 teaspoon sesame oil
1 more teaspoon soy sauce

Combine all of the ingredients except the sesame oil and the 1 teaspoon of soy sauce. Place in a deep bowl and steam for 25 minutes. The eggs will cause the custard to rise like a soufflé. Garnish with sesame oil and soy sauce. Serve immediately.

VARIATION: Instead of minced beef, substitute chopped shrimp, chicken, or well-scrubbed cherrystone clams in their shells. The clams will open as the eggs cook.

Almond Cookies

1 cup sugar
1 cup fresh lard
1 egg
1½ teaspoons baking powder

¼ teaspoon salt
3 cups flour
3 tablespoons almond extract
1 cup blanched whole almonds

Heat the oven to 350° and grease 2 cookie sheets. Cream together the sugar and lard. Add the egg and stir well. Mix in the baking powder and salt, and then the flour and almond extract. Mix well. The dough is rather stiff. With your hands, make little balls of dough about the size of small walnuts. Place the balls on the cookie sheets and flatten them a little with your fingers. The cookies should be thick, and they will spread a little. Press an almond into the center of each cookie. Bake for about 10 minutes or until lightly browned. Cool on a rack.

Note: Butter is rarely used in Chinese cooking.

Honeyed Apples

A dessert to make after dinner.

3 fairly large, crisp apples
Peanut oil for deep-frying
1 egg, beaten
1 cup instantized flour
½ cup water
Pinch cinnamon

½ cup sugar
2 tablespoons honey
⅛ teaspoon powdered ginger
Pinch salt
Ice water

Have an oiled platter and a bowl of ice water ready.

Peel and core the apples. Divide each into eighths. Heat the peanut oil for deep-frying. Mix the egg, flour, water, and cinnamon to make a batter. When the deep-fry oil reaches 350°, dip the apples in the batter, then deep-fry until golden brown. Keep in warm (350°) oven until the syrup is done. In a large, heavy saucepan, mix the sugar, honey, ginger, and salt. Stir over low heat; trickle in enough peanut oil to moisten the mixture. Continue stirring until the sugar dissolves and forms a syrup. Gently stir the apples into the syrup. With tongs or chopsticks, remove the apple slices to an oiled platter. At the table, slices of apple are removed from the platter and dipped into the ice water, briefly. The syrup becomes hard and crisp while the apples inside stay warm and soft. Yummm.

Filling For Sweet Wontons

½ cup dates, chopped
1 tablespoon peanut butter

Pinch of salt
Powdered sugar

Mix and knead all ingredients well. Wrap in Spring Roll Skins (see recipe on page 55), cut to 3-inch size. Wrap either as you would wontons or spring rolls. Deep-fry, drain, and sprinkle with powdered sugar.

Doughnuts

2 eggs, beaten
1 cup light brown sugar
1 teaspoon salt
1 teaspoon baking soda
½ teaspoon allspice

1½ cups buttermilk
3 cups whole wheat flour
Peanut oil for deep-frying
Powdered sugar (optional)

Beat the eggs until light and frothy. Add the light brown sugar, a little at a time, until thick and smooth. Add the salt, baking soda, and allspice to the buttermilk, and add to the sugar mixture. Mix well. Stir in enough flour so that the dough can be handled. Heat deep-fry peanut oil in the wok. Roll out the dough, about ½-inch thick, on a floured board. Cut with a doughnut cutter. Fry doughnuts in deep fat, 2 or 3 at a time. Drain. Dust with powdered sugar if desired.

Barbara's Plum Sauce

12 fresh plums, skinned, stoned, and mashed

1 box dried apricots, minced

1 apple, skinned, cored, and minced

3 peaches, stoned, skinned, and mashed

1 cup cider vinegar

2 cups sugar

½ cup chopped pimiento

Mash all the fruit together. Add the rest of the ingredients and bring to a boil. Barely simmer for 1½ hours. Refrigerate, freeze, or seal in airtight jars. Refrigerate after opening. This sauce continues to improve after it has aged several weeks.

Sweet And Sour Sauce

½ cup sugar
⅓ cup ketchup
1 14 - ounce can pineapple
    chunks, drained and liquid
    reserved

⅓ cup cider vinegar
½ teaspoon garlic powder
2 tablespoons cornstarch
    combined with ⅓ cup
    cold water

Mix the sugar, ketchup, pineapple juice, vinegar, and garlic powder together in a wok. Stir and bring to a boil. Stir in the cornstarch paste and stir until sauce is thickened. Add pineapple chunks just before serving. They should only be heated through—not cooked.

Sukiyaki

One of Japan's best exports.

1½ pounds beef, thinly sliced
1 head bok choy, greens and
   stems sliced separately
6-8 Chinese black dried
   mushrooms, soaked,
   steamed, and sliced

1 large onion, sliced thin
1 can shirataki (yam threads),
   drained
10 scallions, cut in 3-inch
   sections

Stock Mixture:

⅓ cup soy sauce
3 tablespoons sugar
¼ cup sake

2 tablespoons chicken stock
¼ cup sesame oil

Arrange the beef and vegetables attractively on two large plates. Combine the stock mixture and divide into two parts. Heat the wok. Add 2 tablespoons of the sesame oil and stir in the meat from one plate; stir occasionally until meat loses its pink color. Stir in one part of the stock mixture. Stir in all the vegetables from one plate and stir well for 1-2 minutes. Cover the wok and lower heat to barely simmering for 5 minutes. Serve with hot rice. Repeat the cooking process with the remaining ingredients.

Tempura

½ pound fresh shrimp, shelled,
    deveined
½ pound scallops, halved
¼ pound fresh asparagus, cut
    into 4-inch pieces
1 large, sweet potato, sliced
    about ¼-inch thick
1 large green pepper cut in strips
1 medium turnip, sliced about
    ¼-inch thick

1 daikon radish
Soy sauce
Lemon
1⅓ cups cold water
1 small can Japanese wasabi
    horseradish
1 egg
Peanut oil for deep-frying
Sesame oil
1¾ cups instantized flour

Arrange the shrimp, scallops, asparagus, sweet potato, green pepper, and turnip on a platter. Grate the daikon radish and place in small bowls; one for each diner. Have a slightly large bowl of soy sauce for each person, and lemon wedges, to be added to the soy sauce if desired. Add water to the wasabi horseradish to make a thick paste, and place a little lump of the paste to one side on each bowl of the daikon radish. Separate the egg, and beat the white until stiff. Heat enough peanut oil for deep-frying, but add ½ cup sesame oil to it for really good flavor. Beat the egg yolk with ½ cup of the cold water and add the flour. Stir in the rest of the cold water. A few lumps are all right. Fold the egg white into the flour mixture. Fry fish and vegetables, dipping each piece into batter and frying a few at a time. **Serve while cooking**—so have rice hot and ready.

Roman Mixed Fry (Fritto Misto)

Much more Italian than pizza!

Batter:

  ¼ cup olive oil
  1 cup instantized flour
  Pinch of salt and pepper

  ¾ cup water
  1 egg white, stiffly beaten

Things to fry:

  Thin slices of veal marinated in
    white wine; thin slices of
    chicken breast marinated in
    dry vermouth
  Italian green beans

  Eggplant
  Squash
  Green peppers
      all cut into bite-sized pieces

Other Ingredients:

  2½ cups peanut oil for
    deep-frying
  Oregano (optional)

  Lemons
  Watercress or parsley

Two hours before serving add the olive oil to the flour, salt, and pepper. Beat in the water to make a very smooth batter. Marinate the veal in white wine and/or the chicken breast in vermouth. (Either or both may be used.) When ready to serve, heat deep-frying oil. Heat oven to warming temperature (about 200°). Fold the stiffly beaten egg white into the batter. Dip ingredients into the batter and deep-fry a few pieces at a time until golden brown. Drain. Keep warm in the oven until all are done. For a special taste, sprinkle a **little** oregano on one of the ingredients, before dipping it in the batter. Arrange the mixed fry on a large platter and garnish with lemons and watercress or parsley.

MAIL ORDER SOURCES FOR CHINESE FOOD

Mon Fong Wo Co., 36 Pell St., New York 13, N. Y.
Sun Sun Co., 340 Oxford St., Boston, Mass.
Tung Hing Lung Inc., 9 Hudson St., Boston, Mass.
Mee Wah Lung Co., 608 H St. N.W., Washington, D.C.
Sam Wah Yick Kee Co., 2146 Rockwell Ave., Cleveland, Ohio
Mee Jun Mercantile Co., 2223 Wentworth Ave., Chicago, Ill.
Sun Chong Lung, 2220 Wentworth Ave., Chicago, Ill.
Wing On, 1005 Race Street, Philadelphia, Pa.
Lun Sing Co., 10 South 8th St., St. Louis, Mo.
Wah Lee Co., 1331 Third Ave., Detroit, Mich.
Kwong On Lung Importers, 686 N. Spring St., Los Angeles, Cal.
Wing Sing Chong Co., 1076 Stockton St., San Francisco, Cal.
Chung Hing, 202 Milam Street, Houston 2, Texas

INDEX

(continued)